Three dimensional papercraft

Three dimensional papercraft

Hilary Cairns

SEARCH PRESS

Introduction

Three dimensional papercraft is the cutting out, shaping and layering of several identical flat prints to create a beautifully realistic picture full of depth, light and shade. The aim is to delicately 'bring to life' the subject matter, embellishing the artist's work by recreating it as a lifelike form, enhancing the shape, depth and character of the original artist's theme.

It is an absorbing pastime and will appeal to anyone who enjoys creating something beautiful from small beginnings. Artistic talent is not necessary since printed cards and paper can be used as a basis, although original designs can be created if desired. It is also fairly inexpensive in terms of material and equipment and the only extras required are time, patience and care. The more of each you lavish upon your picture the better the end result will be, and excellent results can be obtained within a relatively short space of time.

This craft is not to be confused with decoupage, which is the art of decorating furniture and other flat surfaces with cut out paper prints; once the prints are in position, several coats of varnish are applied to the decorated surface, so that the prints appear to be inlaid. The three dimensional technique explained in this book takes decoupage a step farther. The pictures are not intended to form part of a montage, but are attractive and appealing in their own right.

Three dimensional papercraft is also known as 'Vu d'optique', which literally translated means 'seen optically', or three dimensionally, although the French name has a more subtle ring to it. Another name, also of French origin, is 'paper tole'. The word 'tole' appears to be a corruption of the original meaning which was a form of ornate metalwork of the eighteenth century. Metalware was formed by beating copper or steel to produce a raised pattern. This was then lacquered, or enamelled, and usually gilded. The word 'tole' describes the raised effect of this craft, and it is still used in French Canada today to describe the metalworking form.

Very little is known about the origins of three dimensional papercraft. It is likely it had its beginnings in France after the appearance of decoupage. The craft gained popularity in the Victorian period when mass-produced printed material was readily available and all sorts of cards could be bought, featuring lace and cut paper decorations. 'Peep shows' made from cut out paper in exaggerated perspective stirred the imagination and cut out three dimensional models became an absorbing hobby for young and old alike. There was considerably more time then, without the distractions of television and other modern diversions, to enjoy hobbies and pastimes. Nowadays, however, this delightful craft is enjoying a revival of popularity.

I have covered all the techniques needed to produce both simple, quick projects and more complex pictures requiring a variety of cutting techniques. The projects shown in this book illustrate all the techniques discussed in the opening section, and can be applied to similar or the same type of pictures. The ultimate achievement is to apply all the techniques learnt to create and capture the natural beauty and realism of the subject you are bringing to life, and when admiring friends compliment you on your three dimensional picture, remember that over two hundred years ago paper cutting was an established art form in Great Britain. A well known exponent of this craft was Amelia Blackburn, whose pictures were cut from different shades of coloured paper and built up from small slivers of the paper. Examples of her work can be seen in the British Museum and once you have mastered the basic techniques, you will be inspired to attain the same standards. Whatever your level of expertise, however, you can enjoy this exciting and unusual papercraft.

***The love letter by Charles Edward Wilson**: this charming scene is brought to life using the techniques described on page 38. The young girl is layered up, adding depth and dimension to the cottage garden.*

Materials

Beautifully illustrated cards, prints and gift wrapping paper can be bought everywhere, and as some, or all of the materials can already be found in the home, a start can be made without too much expense. The equipment required is minimal and to make it simple the items are listed with comments, or a description, as appropriate.

Pictures

Several copies of the same card, print or image are required to make a realistic three dimensional picture. Six copies is the ideal minimum but more may be required on very complex pictures. The reason for so many is explained in the section on 'Techniques', (see page 13). Most greetings or birthday cards are suitable, as are prints and wrapping paper. The subject for design should have well-defined edges, which simplifies cutting out. Watercolour-wash paintings are not suitable as there are no easy lines to follow.

If you are a skilled artist you may prefer to create your own three dimensional picture and this can be very satisfying. If you are not too sure of your skill at this stage, an example of a simple design is shown on page 20, with particular reference to the type of paper required.

The choice of paper has a direct bearing on the final result. The thinner the paper the more careful you must be not to crease it; the thicker the card the harder it will be to curve and shape and very thick, glossy printed card creases easily. Never choose a card with an embossed surface as the paper has already been through a shaping process, and any further shaping you may wish to incorporate may not be compatible.

The following section in this book deals with subjects and their suitability for design, (see page 9). Not all subjects lend themselves to this craft and it is recommended that you read this section carefully before making your selection, especially if you have never attempted the craft before. I have included a number of projects in the final section of the book, as examples of how to approach different subjects. The techniques illustrated can be applied to pictures containing the same, or similar, subjects.

Craft tool

It is important to shape each cut-out section of your chosen picture to add depth and life to the subject, and it is the craft, or modelling tool that shapes these sections. A leather working tool is ideal for this

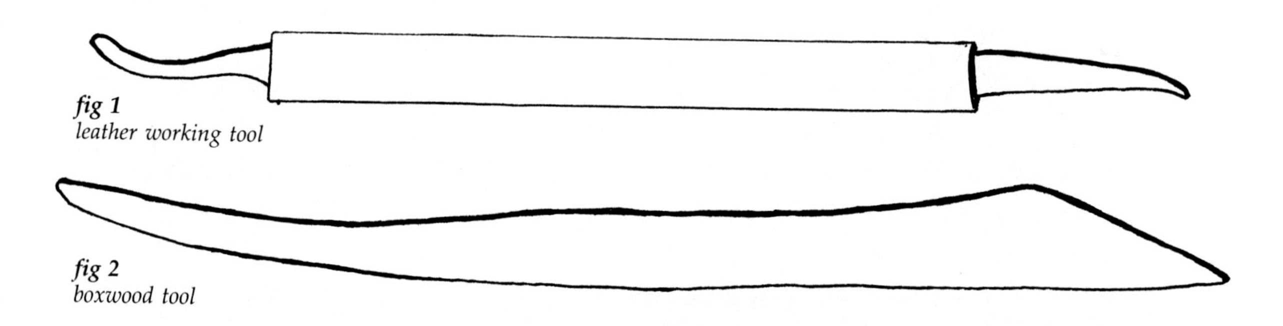

fig 1
leather working tool

fig 2
boxwood tool

purpose, and although not widely available, it can be obtained from suppliers of leather crafting tools or some craft shops. The tool works on paper exceptionally well and is now sometimes sold specifically for three dimensional papercraft. It is double-ended with a straight, plastic tubular handle in the centre. The illustration shows the actual size, (see Fig 1). At one end is an upward curving leaf-shaped spatula, the edges of which are rounded. At the opposite end is a blunt pointed spike. The spatula is used for shaping all cut edges, folds in fabric, petals and so on; the pointed end is rarely used and then only with great care to accentuate details that cannot be cut out, such as small buttons, eyes or jewellery.

Also suitable is the boxwood tool normally used for modelling clay, (see Fig 2). It is widely available, inexpensive and easy to handle. As with the leather working tool, the clay modelling tool is double-ended. At one end is the spatula which is concave on the upper surface and convex below, curving up to a rounded point. Make sure that your tool is wooden, (not plastic), and of good quality as it is important for the spatula to be completely smooth. The handle in the centre is oval and smooth, tapering to a point at the other end. These tools are available in various sizes. The illustration shows the size of the tool used to create the pictures in this book, but a tool with wider 'foot' sections at both ends can also be used.

If you have difficulty in obtaining either of the tools mentioned then seek out alternatives. Household objects such as a teaspoon bowl, or suitably shaped handle, can be used to shape the work and blunt round-ended tapestry needles, or knitting needles, could be used to accentuate fine details that cannot be cut out, or look for alternatives in your local craft shop. In choosing your tool you should look out for the following criteria:

1) A tool with an upward curving spatula shaped end is essential for good shaping, the ideal width of the spatula being approximately ¼in/6mm.
2) A round section shaft such a pencil, or short length of ¼in/6mm dowelling can be used for shaping larger pieces of paper.
3) A pointed tool is necessary for very detailed work. Be sure that the tool you choose has a blunt, rounded point, otherwise you will damage the paper.
4) Finally, make sure tool edges are smooth, otherwise they can crease and tear the paper and ruin all your efforts. It is easier to be accurate with a tool that does not catch on the paper, but flows smoothly over it.

Scissors

One pair of good quality curved nail scissors is required. It is difficult to cut fine detail or "feather" edges with blunt scissors and ragged edges spoil the whole effect of the picture. Sharp scissors are essential for cutting the paper edges cleanly and evenly, so keep this pair specifically for your three dimensional work. Curved scissors allow you to see what you are cutting and are better for working round shapes and angles. Always work with the curve of the blades cutting away from the subject.

If you decide to start by using large, detailed prints, or your own design, (see page 21), an ordinary pair of straight, short-bladed, sharp scissors are more suitable, as curved nail scissors cannot produce long, straight cuts on large paper sections.

Craft knife

A sharp craft knife can be used instead of scissors. However, in this case, I have found it is better to use a good quality cutting mat, preferably a self-sealing mat where old cutting out grooves do not affect future cutting work. The disadvantage of the craft knife is that you are always having to cut down on to a flat surface, whereas with scissors paper can be manoeuvred easily and quickly.

Glue

The type of glue used for this craft is bath and sink sealant, which is widely available from DIY shops. Coloured glue tends to show through the paper so make sure you buy the colourless variety.

If children are eager to participate in this craft, it is advisable for them to use an acrylic based sealant or even self-adhesive pads, rather than a silicone glue. Acrylic sealants are water based, so the paper should be fairly thick, and if used on glazed cards or prints it will affect the paper by leaving an indentation on the surface when dry.

If the tube has a plastic dispensing nozzle, cut a small aperture before you start, to give a better control of the glue. After a bit of practice you may find you prefer to use a wider aperture. It is easier to work with a tube rather than the large pump-action dispensers often available, as you have more control over the flow of the glue. An incautious pump with a dispenser can bathe your hard work in a sticky morass which is impossible to clean off.

Always replace the cap, even when gluing your picture, as the glue seals very quickly. Unless you are meticulous about replacing the cap after each application you will find that the glue has solidified in the tube.

Pencil

A soft leaded pencil is required to shade cut paper edges, for no matter how carefully you cut your paper a visible white edge remains. Grade 2B is recommended. When you are more familiar with the craft you can also use felt-tipped pens to match the colours in your picture. Beware, however, of the paper soaking up the ink and ruining sharp cut edges. It is wise to test for paper absorbency on a scrap piece before shading cut edges with a felt-tipped pen.

Tooth picks or cocktail sticks

These small pointed sticks are invaluable for delicately manipulating the glue to ensure it is put in the right place and in the correct amount.

Working mat

The pieces of cut-out card or paper are shaped on a working mat. This should be of a slightly compressible but resilient material—cork is not suitable as it compresses too much. A beer mat from your local pub, (a clean one!), is ideal, although this size is only suitable for small projects. If you need a larger mat, picture mounting card or a slightly padded plastic table mat are both suitable. Just remember that the mat should give slightly, so that when you press down with the shaping tool on to the paper the tool should sink slightly into the surface. This will impart a curve to the cut-out paper pieces. If the mat is too soft it will compress too much and might crease the paper.

Tweezers

Eyebrow, or stamp collectors' tweezers, are ideal. They are used to handle small paper pieces and to place them in position. They also help to keep the work clean and undamaged, as too much handling can discolour the pieces and tear the edges.

Subjects for design

The subject matter is limitless and you can create your own original designs, but you must adhere to certain guidelines. The outlines of the subject need to be clearly defined, therefore a watercolour wash picture is not suitable as there are no easy cutting lines to follow.

It must be emphasized that embossed pictures are unsuitable as the paper has already been through a shaping process which may not be compatible with the definition you want to incorporate. Gift wrapping-paper, greetings cards and prints are all suitable materials. The thinner the paper the more careful you must be not to crease it; the thicker the card the harder it is to curve and shape.

What follows is a general description of various subject categories and points to watch out for when selecting a picture. Each picture has its own characteristics and peculiarities, and this is where you must combine your interpretation of the subject with the techniques shown in this book, thus imparting a personal touch to the finished item.

Birds

Birds are a marvellous subject and worth spending time over. Beautifully realistic effects are achieved by simply "feather-cutting" edges, (see page 14). The more detail incorporated into the picture, the better your results will be. When final touches are completed it is hard to believe the feathers are not real!

It is best to begin with a fledgling. Although a fair amount of "feathering" is required to give a soft, downy look, not as many sections need to be cut out. Make sure the background to your picture is not too complicated, so you can concentrate on the subject.

You need to study the picture to assess the sections most suitable for cutting out. The secret of success is in the feather cutting. Always feather cut overlapping edges as this will give a complete and beautifully realistic look.

As a guide, the head is usually cut at the neck ruff. Cut along the line of the neck feathers and then feather cut the edge so that the join between the head and body is hardly noticeable. The beak and the eyes are cut out separately unless they are deeply set. If the eyes are deep set, as in the case of an owl they look better just shaped from the back.

Work down the bird's body, following definite colour changes, feather sizes and patterns, even

Pulling a pint by Dick Millington: *Six cards are required to recreate this pub scene. There are no hard and fast rules about the amount of depth you create in your picture, but it is wise to bear in mind the general perspective the artist intends to portray. Layer from the back to the front and refer to the "Techniques" section commencing on page 13 for guidance.*

The details beyond the two "locals" in the doorway are indistinct, so begin by cutting out these figures and gluing them on the main base card.

The open doorway into the crowded bar gives a lovely feeling of depth, so now cut out the front of the pub, carefully cutting around the door frame. The glowing yellow light of the window is cut out, so the frame stands proud of the base picture when this section is glued in position. Details such as the snow covered door porch, step, bay window and pub sign could all be cut out, shaped and layered to add to the feeling of depth. Cut out each member of the band individually, rather than as a group.

individual feathers. The wings are best cut into four sections, starting with the feathers at the base of the wing; cut out individual feathers for even more effect. Layer the legs, chest area and tail separately; the latter two can often be cut into more sections, particularly on a bird like the tawny owl where there are definite band markings.

Animals

I have found that animals do not always provide good results. The natural lines of smooth coated animals are difficult to reproduce, as there are no definite cutting lines or breaks in the body outline. As an example, if you cut out the leg of a dog, then shape and glue it into position, it appears that the leg is a separate entity, rather than part of the whole animal.

Long haired animals are easier to tackle as cut lines can be obscured by "feathering" edges, (see page 14). The cat family is particularly suitable, and stunningly realistic three dimensional pictures can be created fairly easily. Be prepared for a great deal of feathering to achieve excellent results!

Figures

Adults and children make attractive and appealing subjects. Folds of clothes, shoes, socks and buttons enhance and enliven a picture when they are cut out and shaped. Ensure that your subject is not too large because it is difficult to reproduce a three dimensional portrait. By shaping the cheeks and nose a face is accentuated, but in close up the overall effect is not sufficiently realistic.

The three dimensional effect is achieved by layering clothing, hair and additional items such as handbags, shopping baskets or toys. These all help to give depth and structure to the picture.

By carefully studying individual positions in groups of people you can bring the scene to life. Build background figures up to only one or two layers thick, or those in the foreground will require so many layers and enormous amounts of glue, that the finished picture will be extremely "thick". This detracts from the overall effect of realism.

Cartoons

Cartoon cards like the one shown opposite offer an amusing and unusually attractive range of subject matter. Outlines are simple and easy to follow, and finished pictures add colour to a child's room.

Flowers

Flowers, with their incredible variety of shapes and colours, are the most beautiful and rewarding of subjects. Simple blossoms with one layer of petals, such as the poppy, primrose or busy lizzie, are excellent subjects for your first attempt, as there is not much depth of perspective in the flower heads.

Begin with a simple print with good, well-defined lines and sharp colours, preferably without a background so you can concentrate on the subject without the added complication of extraneous features. This simple project will allow you to develop your technique and yet obtain beautiful results without taking too much time. Once you have completed your first three dimensional flower you will soon feel confident enough to undertake more detailed flowers, such as roses or peonies.

Always take time to study the flower, seeking out the back petals first. Beware of petals that curve round from background to foreground as these will have to be "over-cut" so they lie successfully under other back petals. Over-cutting is described along with other cutting methods in the section on "Techniques", (see page 15). As a guide, the following steps should be taken when creating a three dimensional flower.

Take one card from the set and cut out the whole flower. Lightly shade cut edges.

Shape by placing the flower face down on the working mat, and with the curved foot of the craft tool, press round the edge in a flowing movement, so the edges curl upwards slightly. When viewed from the front the petal will curve away from you. If the picture shows the petal with a definite upward curve, then gently shape it upwards with your fingers, or round the central handle of the tool.

Take another card and over-cut out the back petal as though the whole petal is visible. This ensures that there are no unsightly edges showing when overlapping petals are laid on top and the three dimensional effect is enhanced.

With a toothpick place a small spot of glue on the corresponding petal of the main base flower and using the tweezers place the cut out petal in position on top of the original. The bottom of the petal should touch the base picture at the centre of the flower, while the outer edge should be raised by the spot of glue approximately 2mm/⅛in. Wait for the glue to dry before continuing with the next layer.

You will only need one layer of back petals. Using all but one of your cards, but using as much of each picture as is possible, gradually build up the petals, always working from the back of the flower to the front in layers and completing each layer before moving on to the next. The flower will slowly start emerging from the flat print, taking on a more realistic form. When the flower has been completed, either glue it on to the unused card, or a mounting board in a contrasting or complementary colour.

Scenes

There are many beautiful cards and prints illustrating this subject. Houses and gardens, trees and fields must be carefully studied before embarking upon a three dimensional scene. Remember, when beginning to create a picture showing great distance, never cut out that distant view, or the glued front sections of the picture will have to be raised so high that all sense of perspective is lost.

General

Water is not a suitable subject. It is difficult to translate a boat scene into three dimensional terms as the boat literally "sits" in the water. If you want to choose water as a subject, select a picture showing waves which have natural cut lines and a definite perspective.

Round, smooth objects are not suitable. Apples and balloons do not always achieve pleasing results, unless they are small and not the main subject of the picture.

Your eye will soon get used to looking at a picture with three dimensions in mind. Buying birthday cards will become a lengthy process, and an enjoyable one. You will often leave the shop with an armful of cards for your hobby, as well as the original birthday card! What better gift for a friend or relative than your own three dimensional picture, with its beauty, realism and depth of perspective.

Techniques

There are four basic stages in three dimensional papercraft: assessment of the picture, cutting out, shaping and gluing. Provided each stage is patiently carried out in its correct sequence, the end result will be attractive and effective.

Assessment of the picture

Each subject has its own characteristics and perspective. After choosing your picture, sit down and study it before making a start. Determine the perspective. Decide which area forms the background and which elements are closest to you. The more you study the picture the more detail you will observe. Work within the limits of the number of identical pictures you have, and assess how much detail you are going to "bring out", bearing in mind that the less detail you incorporate, the flatter the finished picture. On the other hand, too much detail can cause the perspective to distort, or you may run out of prints from which to take your cut pieces.

It is easier to decide on the amount of detail to use if the picture contains only a single subject, e.g., a rose; but even with a single rose it is essential to determine the number of layers required to create the right perspective. Depending on the angle and viewpoint, the outside petals of a rose will be closer to you than the centre of the flower, whereas with the front view of a bird, the beak is nearest to you.

If the picture is scenic, decide how much of the background, if any, should be built up. If the background is too distant, do not use it in the actual building up process. Never cut out the distant view, as the glued front sections of the picture would have to be raised so high that to retain the correct balance, all sense of perspective would be lost. The overall effect would be spoilt because the excessively raised foreground would look clumsy and unattractive.

The one subject which does not lend itself to this idea of perspective is the close front view of a face. It is difficult to reproduce a three dimensional portrait, and it is far better to create a whole figure, in which case the perspective is obvious.

Never stop studying your picture. Try to see it as a real, living scene and take each item, from the farthest point away to the nearest point, step by step in the building up process. If you look at the picture as a whole you may feel intimidated by the detail and work involved. But by following the step by step process of assessment, cutting, shaping and gluing, you will suddenly discover that your work will begin to take shape. Out of the flat image will emerge a beautiful three dimensional picture. This, more than anything else, will inspire you to attempt more detailed and complex subjects.

Summary

1. Decide on the natural perspective, i.e., that part of the subject which would be closest to you if it was real.
2. Look for the object - petal, leaf, feather, branch, etc., that would be farthest away from you. Decide whether this object is too much in the distance and therefore not suitable for cutting out, or whether it is sufficiently close to warrant its own layer.

Cutting out

Always keep one of your cards intact as a backing on to which to paste the finished picture and as a reference when cutting out. Alternatively you can glue the finished picture on to plain backing card or mounting board.

Precise cutting out is important; follow outlines accurately and re-check your intact backing card whenever you are unsure of a line that looks as though it is blending with the background. It is better to take longer and to cut out accurately than to discover that a section has been cut in error. If a cutting error has been made there are two solutions. You can either cut out the section for later layering up in the same way, or use a new card discarding the damaged card for later stages.

Because most lines are curved, remember that you need curved blades on your scissors, as these allow you to see what you are cutting. Make sure the scissors are sharp and always cut out with the blades working away from the outside edges of the design. This produces a fine bevelled edge, so less of the cut white edge shows.

When starting, always cut out the main subject. If it is a rose, or any subject on a blank background, then the whole subject should be cut out. If it is a scene that will be built up on the backing card, the first item to cut out is the one that would appear farthest away in reality. This way the picture is gradually built up. Be careful! It is not advisable to cut every section out and then build up a picture, but to constantly assess, cut out a section, shade and shape, and then glue into position.

Items at the back of the picture usually only have one layer placed on the original backing picture. For example, if the back item is a rose petal, one back petal is cut out and glued in place on to the main flower head background.

In the case of the front view of a bird, it is the tail or body which forms the single layer background. You may decide to leave the tail only on the background sheet and make the body the first layer. Front sections usually have a maximum of four layers, unless feather cutting is employed.

If you are cutting out a section from the centre of a picture, resist the temptation to cut in from the edge to reach it. Always cut out with the minimum of damage to the rest of the picture.

There are several cutting out techniques and each has its own application. Before you begin to cut you should decide which technique is suitable for your picture.

Straight cutting

The most common type of cutting is the straight cut line. It is used for straight edged items such as rose petals or cartoon subjects. The cut follows the outline of the design without any need to soften the edge.

Feather cutting

Feather cutting enhances a picture and gives it greater realism. This type of cut is not only used for feathers but for hair, fur and any edging that requires a ragged, uneven look. Subjects with fluid smooth

An example of feather cutting is shown above.

lines are normally difficult to reproduce three dimensionally, but if they have feathers or long fur they are most suitable, as a feather cut edge will cover what would otherwise be straight cut layered lines.

To begin, cut out the section, broadly following the outline of the design. Then cut into the edge of the paper, as if you were cutting a 'V' shape, with straight and angled cuts of different lengths. It is most important that these cuts differ in size, length and angle, yet adhere to the subject outline as much as possible. The final 'ragged' edge makes feathers and fur look incredibly realistic and it also makes paper shaping easier at rounded outside edges. Use a wider spaced cut for fur and a close cut for feathers, hair or grasses, keeping the cuts in proportion to the size of the subject. Never be tempted to pull paper sections out after feather cutting. If the cuts have not met accurately, there will be an obvious torn edge which is difficult to shade.

Textured cutting

This is suitable for woolly, textured or lacy edges and involves small, undulating cuts along the edge of the paper. Use the scissors in a close "in and out" rounded motion with a curving finish, as opposed to a ragged or feathered finish. This imparts a softer outline to the design.

Circular cutting

When cutting out a circular object, be very careful to extend the cutting motion, keeping it as long as possible. Small short cuts leave tiny pointed edges that need to be snipped off afterwards, so reducing your chances of having an accurately sized section left to work with.

Over-cutting

Over-cutting is a most important part of the three dimensional process, and is essential for obtaining a proper perspective. It simply means that in cutting out background sections which are to be overlaid by other sections, an allowance must be made on the inner edge of the design, that is, the area nearest the centre of the picture. In other words cut out more than is required; the next piece will hide the overcut section and hide harsh cut lines.

Cut inner edges 1/6 to 1/8 in / 2 to 4mm larger than the actual outline. Try to envisage the outline of the background piece as though it is not obscured and cut out the hidden section as if it exists. Visible edges are cut true to the picture. The reason for doing this is that in the effort to reproduce reality, the subject has to be treated as though all parts of it are whole. For example, a petal should be cut out so that the outside edge is true to the picture, but make sure that the covered inner portion of the petal is cut larger than it is. This means you are cutting into other petals, as though the whole of the petal is visible. Over-cutting ensures that when overlapping petals are laid on top of each other, there are no unsightly edges and therefore the total three dimensional effect is enhanced.

Summary

There are two important points to remember about the cutting out process.

1. Never cut through the design unless you have to. If you are cutting out a section from the centre of the picture, resist the temptation to cut in from the edge to reach it. Always cut out with the minimum of damage to the rest of the picture. One of the easiest mistakes to make is to cut through sections unnecessarily when requiring just a portion of a subject, only to discover later on that all the pieces have been cut through, and there are no cards left to work on!
2. When cutting out sections of the picture for use in the building up process, always check that cut pieces can be taken from another card for use later on.

Shading

Use a soft pencil to lightly shade cut paper edges, so no visible white edges remain. If the shading is too dark the edges will stand out and spoil the finished effect. Felt-tipped pens to match colours in the picture can be used but test for paper absorbency on a scrap piece before shading. When shading feather-cut edges, draw the pencil along the feathered edge in a light brush-stroke movement.

Shaping

Shaping is an important step in achieving dimension and perspective. It adds subtle depth and realism to the picture. No matter how good the cutting out, without the shaping the picture will remain lifeless and dull - just paper cut-outs sandwiched together with glue.

Curves give height to your pictures and it is important to only shape the outside edges of all pieces. Because of these outside curves, the centre of the cut piece will automatically lift up and cut outlines will be disguised.

To shape particular sections of a picture is simple. To begin, place the cut-out piece *face down* on your working mat. Using the craft tool 'foot', press down and draw the 'foot' around the cut edge. Never use the tool 'foot' on the right side of the paper and never over-press or hurry or you may crease the paper. The result you are looking for is a gentle curve upwards, so that when viewed from the front the cut-out edges bend away from you very slightly.

When shaping larger sections, use the tool stem, or tweezers, or your fingers to curl the paper, but do not bend the paper too much as creases are liable to appear. Try not to change your mind about which way you want something shaped, as once it is done it is impossible to reverse curves without damage.

The amount of pressure required varies with the type of mat you are working on and the type of paper or card, but as a general rule it is much better to shape a few times gently than exert too much pressure at once. If the paper becomes creased, (something to try to avoid), place the cut-out section face down on the mat and gently work the tool 'foot' around in a circular motion. You will find that the crease will almost disappear.

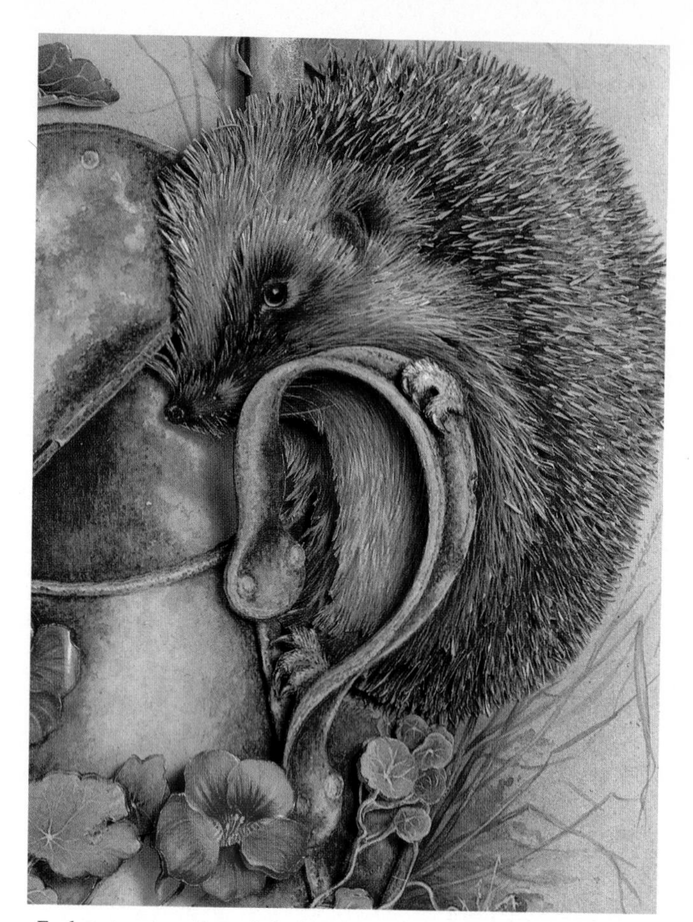

Each cut out section of the hedgehog is shaped before it is glued on to the base picture.

Study your design and think about the shapes you are following. Flower petals should have soft, shaped edges; birds and animals have round forms and their edges should lie on the background picture.

Leaf veins can be enhanced beautifully by shaping. Hold the cut-out leaf up to the light, wrong side towards you, and with a pencil gently mark the vein line. Place the leaf face down on the working mat and with the tool 'foot' slightly angled on its side, press down, drawing it along the pencil line. When the leaf is turned over the vein will stand out.

If you want to accentuate the fold of a piece of material, hold the section up to the light and mark the fold with a pencil, as with the leaf vein. However, when you start shaping, press the tool 'foot' on *either side* of the pencil line. When the paper section is turned over, the fold itself is concave and each side of the fold is convex.

When shaping minute details, such as buttons, stones, eyes or flower centres, repeat the technique for marking the wrong side of the cut-out section and with the tool spike gently press down to accentuate the various details.

When shaping stems, tails and branches, or anything that is long and tubular, bear in mind that once it has been shaped it will no longer be the same size as the picture on the backing sheet. This is usually not noticeable when the item is raised up and away from the backing card by glue. However, this is not always the case! So never fix anything in place until you have first checked how it is going to look when glued to the backing card. Do this by placing the unglued section over the corresponding image on the backing card. If it does not look correct it may be because it has been shaped too much, or in the case of a flower it may need the insertion of an additional petal or leaf. This is easy to achieve by cutting an extra petal and inserting it into the gap, even if it does not appear in the actual picture. If there is no petal available you can easily make one up, using a similarly coloured section from one of the used cards.

Gluing

The type of glue best suited to this craft is a bath and sink sealant. It should always be applied to the paper with a toothpick or cocktail stick. These small pointed sticks are invaluable for delicately manipulating the glue to ensure that it is put in the right place and in the correct amount.

Always clear your working area before commencing and keep the section you are about to glue in position near at hand. An important point to remember is that only small portions of glue are needed. Never cover the area that is about to be layered with vast amounts of glue. Depending on the size of the cut-out section you will rarely need a spot of glue smaller than a lentil or larger than a baked bean! For larger areas, two or three spots of glue may be required, rather than one large blob. Keep the glue away from edges so that it will not squash out during the layering process and become visible. When gluing a long stem, or tail etc., only place a spot of glue at either end. If it does not lie well on top of the corresponding layer beneath, a touch of glue carefully placed in the middle should solve the problem.

Place the glue on to the backing card, or layer that is about to be covered. Never place it on to the section about to be positioned. If the card or paper has a glossy surface, make sure the glue is not inadvertently spilt on an uncovered layer. The glue will permanently mark the gloss finish. With the help of tweezers, (especially if you are positioning a small piece of paper), gently ease the cut-out section into position. As the glue takes several minutes to dry, you can tilt the section to whatever angle you wish - either to right and left or up and down, whichever looks right. You may need to compress the section slightly if it appears too high up in relation to the layer beneath.

Do not rush this stage as it can end in disaster. Once one piece has been stuck down do not attempt to stick adjacent pieces down until the glue has completely dried.

If a section has been positioned and a mistake been made, or you are not happy with the angle, then take the following action. Allow the glue to dry completely, then carefully snip it in two using the small nail scissors. If the paper is glossy the glue may peel off the section that has been removed. You can now replace it in the correct position. If the glue does not peel off, not as much will be needed because the padding is already there. It may be, however, that you will have to replace the original cut-out section with a new piece.

Sarah's cat by Sarah Adams: *The simple lines and the subject make this project an excellent example for illustrating different techniques. Five cards are needed and the first card forms the main base picture. Cut out the floral curtain, over-cutting where necessary and not forgetting the small area protruding from the open window. Shade edges and shape folds. Glue in position.*

The open window and hanging fuchsia are the next items to be cut out. Use a craft knife to cut the wooden window frame. Darkening and shaping edges is important, even though the frame is light-coloured and straight. Glue in position.

The ginger cat is cut out in one piece and not layered up at all. Accentuate the eyes and nose and shape around the edges. Feather cut around furry edges. The front legs and rear foot will benefit from shaping. The geranium is rather detailed, but you can cut out the whole plant and pot, as I have, slightly accentuating details by cutting out a few spaces and back leaves.

The final section requires the craft knife again. Cut out the closed window sill, but when shaping the frame do not let the paper edges bend over too much. Shape so that they curve over slightly. The whole section will tend to bend after shaping, so build it up with glue to keep the frame upright and uniform.

Creating your own picture

A columbine, has been used to illustrate how effective an original design can be, but any subject would be suitable, providing outlines are clearly defined and simple. If you do not keep the subject simple you may find that items overlap, causing problems when layering up. The design is sketched out first. Different coloured papers have been used to create the columbine and this is an easy and attractive way of enhancing the depth of a picture. Choose colours carefully so they blend and match.

The columbine drawing below was photocopied on to several coloured sheets of paper which were cut out, shaped and layered in the same way as the printed cards. Shaping has to be accentuated if using coloured paper, as the colours do not contain the subtle nuances of light and shade that can be seen in a printed picture.

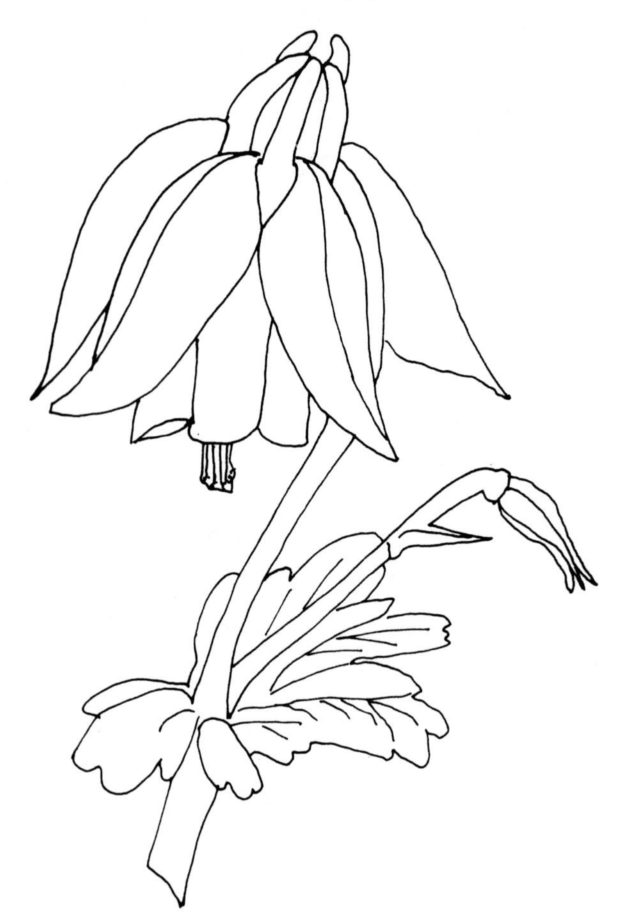

When creating your own design choose good quality flexible card or paper. This is very important, otherwise you may find that "shaping" and "creasing" seem to go hand in hand! On low grades of paper the glue has a tendency to show on the right side of the surface. A paper weight of 150gsm or above is a suitable thickness.

Work out your basic drawing and transfer it on to the paper. It is easier to photocopy the original drawing the required number of times, using coloured paper if desired, but if a photocopier is not available the drawing has to be transferred on to the required number of sheets. Make a template of your original drawing and copy it out as needed. If using a photocopier avoid the paper provided as it is not suitable and make sure the machine will accept your paper or card. Also, check that the copy ink is fixed on to your paper surfaces. If colouring your picture do not use poster paints, or any finish that will crack when cutting and shaping. Markers or felt pens are suitable as they will not run if you want to varnish your finished picture. It will not be necessary to colour each and every copy of the drawing as only certain sections will be used. Colour as you go along in the building up process.

Finishing touches

You should now feel confident with the pictures you are creating and will want to display them in the best possible way. A contrasting mount and an attractive frame will enhance your picture and give it the final finishing touch.

A simple, inexpensive and effective way of

***Columbine by Hilary Cairns**: an easy and attractive way to enhance the three dimensional effect of an original design is to use a variety of coloured papers. Here, the colours have been chosen carefully so they blend and match.*

finishing off your picture is to mount it on a mounting board. This type of board is very thick card, slightly thicker than a beer mat and is available from any art shop or picture framer. The surface is covered with coloured paper overlaid on white compressed card. Whenever you cut out the size you need, it must be larger than your finished picture, so that you have an attractive mount surrounding the subject. Measure very accurately, preferably using a metal ruler, and cut the mount with a very sharp craft knife, or universal cutter that has changeable blades. Always try to use new blades, wiped clean as they are often greased to prevent rusting. You will then have clean smooth cut edges to your board. Glue your picture on to the mount board with a paper glue.

Two contrasting mounts can be used to make an attractive and effective frame. Glue your picture on to one of the mounts and use the other mount as a frame, positioning it *over* the picture. This top 'frame' can be raised up using self-adhesive sticky pads, but be careful how you use them, because once in place, they are there for all time!

To frame a three dimensional picture, a box frame is ideal, as its depth will encompass your picture and the glass will stand proud of your work. You can frame the picture without glass, but be careful when dusting it because of its delicate nature! You may find your picture framer does not have a suitable box frame, but one can be built up by using two frames, one on top of the other, to give the necessary depth.

Varnishing is another way of finishing off your picture to great effect. The final result gives a finish similar to glazed china. There are two things to remember; firstly the glazed finish on many cards does away with any need for varnishing, particularly if the picture is to be shown under glass when complete; secondly, varnishing will give the picture a slightly beige look.

Varnishing is a very effective method to use on items that are not intended as wall hangings. For example, items which are regularly handled such as box lids, or fridge magnets, are given additional strength with three or four sprayed layers of varnish. Do be sure to use a spray-on varnish for an even application, following the directions on the can.

Cottage garden by John H. Tyson: *A natural frame sets this picture off beautifully. For details of how to build up the cottage garden,* *see page 45.*

Projects

All the techniques shown earlier in the book are used to create the pictures on the following pages. Use these examples as a basis for your pictures. Simple and more complex pictures are illustrated covering a wide range of subjects. Beautiful three dimensional objects make lovely gifts for friends and relatives and the simple ideas described on this page are ideal for the beginner.

Gift tags, decorated boxes, pictures, festive table decorations, or just special birthday and get-well cards, are ideal first projects if you are thinking of taking up this craft. A plain box adorned with a simple, pretty three dimensional flower, looks charmingly different and rather special. It could be used as gift wrapping and can be prepared in advance. Why not make a whole range of three dimensional Christmas "stick-ons" just in case there is no time left to wrap those last minute presents!

A beautiful butterfly refrigerator magnet created out of used cards makes a lovely small gift for a friend or neighbour. The finished butterfly illustrated here has been sprayed with clear varnish three times to make it strong and durable - make sure the first coat of varnish is dry before you apply the next coat.

These ideas can be used as a springboard for your own projects. A paperweight is an attractive gift and easy enough for a child to do. Varnish a simple three dimensional flower and glue it on to a painted and glazed stone. Mix colours and themes in a room by using matching wallpaper to build up pictures that can be framed. Creating three dimensional pictures or objects from a flat image is inexpensive and fun to do. All you need is time, patience and a little care.

Details from the picture illustrated on page 27: *details of used cards can be cut out and layered up. The three dimensional potentilla shown opposite can be used to adorn a special present. The butterfly has been made into a simple refrigerator magnet. Glue the butterfly to a small magnet with strong-drying ahesive and strengthen with several coats of varnish.*

Teddy bear

This simple study in perspective is a perfect picture for a child's nursery. Six identical cards are needed.

As with all my three dimensional pictures, it is important to assess the subject carefully before commencing. Cut out the whole picture of the bear, telephone receiver and cord. The layers are built up on this base. The soft, furry outline of the teddy bear can be enhanced by cutting a slightly curved, undulating edge around the body. Carefully cut away the background between the telephone receiver and the head. Darken cut edges with a soft leaded pencil; this stops the white cut line from showing.

The next important step is the shaping. Place the bear face down on your working mat, and with the craft tool foot press down, moving it slowly around the cut edges so they curl up slightly. When viewed from the front, the cut edges should bend away from you.

Take another complete picture. Study it and note which sections would be farthest away if the bear was real. In this case it is the ears. Over-cut the ears This means cutting through any part of the picture lying over the section you are cutting out as if all areas of the ears are visible. Unless it is an outside edge, cut the section slightly larger. Remember to make textured cuts around the edges. Darken the cut edge as before and shape with the tool foot.

Place a spot of glue on to each ear of the teddy bear base. Carefully, with the aid of some tweezers, place each ear in position on top of the glue. The ears can be gently manipulated with the tweezers, as the glue takes several minutes to dry. Tilt the outside of each ear up so that the inside edge, next to the head, touches the base. Make sure that the head and telephone receiver outlines form a continuous line.

Take another card and seek out the next section for layering. In this case it is the top half of the telephone receiver. Over-cut the receiver . Shade, shape and glue into position, matching outlines and

***Teddy bear by Glücki**: this lovable teddy simply illustrates the techniques required to create an appealing three dimensional picture.*

making sure the first layer of glue is completely dry before sticking the next layer down.

Cut out the bear's head, but omitting the ears. Take another unused card and over-cut the whole face as if all of it was visible, texturing the edge. When shaping, accentuate the roundness by gently curving edges over the tool. Glue the head in position, tilting the top outwards and the nose down towards the base.

If you want to add extra perspective to the face, you can cut out the white snout, eyes and nose. Here, just the black nose has been cut out. Over-cut the nose, darken the edges and glue it gently in position, tilting it down towards the telephone receiver. Over-cut the paw holding the receiver, taking the picture from one of the previously used cards, shade, shape and glue it in position. Over-cut the legs from one of the used cards. Shade and shape, but when gluing the legs on to the body attach the feet with a larger portion of glue than the legs, so that they are higher and the top of the legs are touching the body.

Cut out the body, over-cutting sections that are not visible. Accentuate the roundness by pressing the tool foot in a circular motion all over the section, so that it is convex when viewed from the right side. Use three pea-sized spots of glue when placing the body in position.

Over-cut the bow; shade, shape, and this time carefully curl the bow ends upwards so, when viewed from the front, they bend away from you.

Over-cut the telephone receiver mouthpiece. Cut out the telephone cord and only over-cut the top where the arm covers the cord. The cord obviously cannot be cut out exactly as it appears in the picture, so either cut it out in much the same way as the bear's outline, or cut two straight lines either side of the cord. Shape and glue the two pieces.

Cut out the feet and bear's right hand arm. Shade, shape and glue in position. Tilt the arm up at the paw, and down at the elbow, before the glue dries.

Finally, decide whether you want to stick your teddy bear down on to a backing card of the same picture, see finished illustration, or glue it on to a coloured mounting board for framing, (see page 22).

Potentilla and butterflies

Although this charming picture looks very difficult, it is not. The only problem is the size of the paper sections with which you are dealing. Naturally, when an item is very small it is difficult to impart minute details of specific shaping or embossing, so the three dimensional effect is achieved by the number of layers and gluing of the subject.

With this example the great contrast of colours means that the layering up process is more natural than, say, the more difficult and muted shades of birds' feathers. To achieve satisfactory results, you will need five cards if you are putting the finished picture on to your own backing, six cards if you are putting the finished picture on to the original picture.

When studying the picture of the potentilla flowers, the distance or nearness of each leaf and flower head will become apparent. So when starting, as always, cut out the whole subject; leaves, flowers, butterflies and even the little ladybird in the foreground. Assess what aspects of the picture are farthest away, as if the flowers were real. When you have made this assessment, at this stage do not cut out these items, or details in the foreground will stand out far too much by the time the gluing and layering up is finished.

Now decide which items would be the second farthest away from you, again studying the flowers as if they were real. This time over cut out the leaves, petals, buds and butterflies, (see page 15 for overcutting).

Three layers have been used for the butterflies: the main base, then one complete butterfly outline and finally the wings and body to give a realistic perspective. Cut out the body, feelers and top section of the wings for the orange and white butterfly, and the lower section of green wing for the green butterfly, shading, shaping and gluing as you layer up (see "Techniques", page 13).

The flowers, on the other hand, have been layered in a different way and you will notice that the petals overlap each other. Only on the larger flowers, and not the flower facing away from you, begin by cutting out the petal that is most overlapped, or that looks farthest away from you. Darken the edges and very slightly shape, then glue in position. Carry on building up the petals until you are only left with the middle stamens. These are rather fiddly to cut out, but so rewarding when glued into place, making the potentillas look beautifully realistic.

***Potentilla and butterflies by Eleanor Ludgate**: a beautifully realistic effect is easily achieved with these simple potentillas, by cutting out and overlapping the petals of each flower head. The pretty butterflies add charm and perspective to the picture.*

Fleur Cowles

Roses with their delicacy, beauty and colours, are one of the most rewarding of subjects. The structure of the flower lends itself to this craft; the many layers of overlapping petals give the picture such depth and form that, in the past, roses I have created have often been mistaken for the real thing!

Seven cards are used and approximately twenty three sections are cut out to create the lovely bloom opposite, but the good thing is that several sections can be worked on at the same time, without waiting for the glue to dry. After finishing this rose I glued it on to a box lid and used several coats of varnish to give it a beautiful, porcelain-like appearance.

Roses are not the easiest of subjects, but the usual rules apply. Details of building up three dimensional flowers are given on page 11. Always start by studying your picture; do not look at it as a whole, but as individual segments, starting at the back and working forward. If you do this you will find a three dimensional form beginning to emerge from the flat image.

Before starting, there are three points to remember. Do not let the glue ooze out of the sides of cut out sections. Shape each piece carefully, especially the petals. If shaping makes the section too small to cover the corresponding image below, do not be afraid to create another petal from an unused section of the picture, matching colour as much as possible. This will give added depth and dimension.

In this instance the final picture does not have a backing card, therefore the whole rose is cut out: leaves, flower head and stem all together in one piece. The edges are darkened with a soft leaded pencil and shaped so that they curve over slightly.

There are four obvious sections at the rear of this picture that need to be cut out, shaded, shaped and glued in position first. These are the petal at the very back of the rose, the thin rose leaf, the fine rose bud leaf, (just under the petals), and the large leaf half hidden by the rose petal. Shaping of sections at the rear of the picture is not as important as sections in the foreground, but do shape petals with care and a little more emphasis, and you will be rewarded when you look at your completed picture.

The next stage is to cut the rose stem and the dark pink petal tucked away in the background. Remember to over-cut sections that will be overlaid later on. Shade, shape and glue in position.

Now cut out the partly obscured bud leaves, the far right hand leaf and the petal third from the back. There are two things to remember here and these, in fact, become part of the fourth stage in the layering up process. Where the leaf has a folded over edge, or as in the case of the bud leaf, where the top half is lighter green and obviously nearer than the dark green area beneath, cut these folded pieces out as a further stage and glue them in position. Think of how a real curled over leaf looks and make sure the actual fold is touching the layer below, slightly lifted up at one side to give some depth and reality.

You will see, as you progress, that you are working from the top and bottom of the picture at the same time and working towards the centre. In this case the centre of the picture is not too obvious. As you can see it is the large, faintly yellow and pink petal with curled over edges. These edges present no problem because you use the same techniques as already described. But this petal does not appear to be the first, or last, to be glued in position. In fact, it is the penultimate section, discounting the curled over edges and water droplets which are added at the final stage. If you look at the outline of the centre petal you will see that the section on the left is naturally in front of the slightly misshapen petal on the far left.

***Fleur Cowles by James Noble**: a box lid makes an unusual mount for this delicately painted rose. The petals are cut out and layered up, then the finished flower is glued on to the lid with strong fast-drying ahesive.*

But, looking at the other side, it is *behind* the curved petal on the right. Although the right-hand petal actually curves round the base of the rose, for the purposes of the three dimensional image, it is better to split it into two separate petals. Fortunately there is an obvious section for a natural cut line, where the light ends and the darker section of petal is in shadow. Cut out these sections, shape and glue in position.

Do not despair while grappling with the many layers and sections in this project. You may feel you are fighting a losing battle! Suddenly, the picture will emerge and your efforts will be rewarded as the beautiful rose takes shape.

Christmas robin

This type of subject is delightful to work on because in the flat picture there is already a three dimensional effect; that of the robin sitting on the holly branch with a distant background of snow and winter woodland. Five cards are required for this picture, which would make a special Christmas card for a member of your family, or a friend, and all the techniques required are shown earlier in the book.

Although it is a fairly detailed subject, because of the holly leaves and the feathers, there is really not a great deal of work to it.

As with all three dimensional pictures, the main subject has to be cut out; in this instance the robin and the holly branch. You may find certain areas are extremely difficult to cut out, for example, the section in between the robin's back and the holly branch and leaf. When you come across similar problems, you must rely on your own judgement, weighing up whether the cut can be executed neatly and without damaging the paper print.

When you have cut out the branch, leaves and robin in one piece, darken the edges with a soft lead pencil. Shaping at this stage and on this particular subject is not really necessary, but in my picture I have shaped the larger sections of leaves and, more importantly, the edges of the robin, so that they curve over slightly. This adds form and depth to the finished picture.

Study the robin carefully; the first section that is over-cut out is the leg in the forefront of the picture. Shade the edges and glue it carefully in position.

The next section is the robin's tail and back feathers. Start cutting out from the base of the head, over-cutting into the wing and right down to the tail feathers. This section will need to be very finely feather cut on exposed edges, (see page 14 for feather cutting techniques). Darken the edges, shape in a slight convex and glue in position.

The white body feathers will need to be cut out now. Over-cut out into the wing feathers and well into the red breast feathers. The difficult cut line from wing to body should be where the very white fluffy feather overlaps the brown wing feathers. Feather cut around the body, darken the edges, even though it is light coloured, and shape in a rounded convex; finally glue in position.

The wing, body and head feathers are next; over-cut out the wing and brown head section in one piece, using the white and red feathers as a cutting guide. Make sure you curve the cuts in and out at the base of the wing, following the feather tips and build up the layers. When shaping this section, also make sure you emphasise the feather lines. Mark the section on the wrong side with lines corresponding to the flight feathers, then draw along the lines with the working tool, pressing fairly heavily so that when

***Christmas robin by Chris Shields**: this little robin is beautifully brought to life by a process of feather cutting and layering. The holly berries and leaves are also cut out and layered to complete the three dimensional effect.*

looked at from the right side there are ridges defining the feather outlines. Darken edges as usual and glue into position.

Cut out the white and red feathers of the head and chest and incorporate the beak. Feather the edges all round, shaping the beak in the same way as the distinctive flight feathers. The eye can also be shaped rather than cutting it out and gluing it into position.

When working on the holly branch, choose only the foreground leaves; cut them out, darken the edges and shape. The shaping is important here. To make the leaves look real, the veins need to be drawn on with the tool and the leaf tips curved up or down with your fingers.

Don't forget to cut out the berries and the moth! If you are feeling enthused with the picture try cutting out some segments of snow; don't glue them into place until you are satisfied that they look correct.

Tawny talk

Birds are a delightful subject for re-creating in a three dimensional way. Stunningly realistic effects can be achieved fairly simply and feather cutting brings out the natural beauty of even the smallest bird. This picture, with its subtle background, stark branches and the fine colouring of the owls, would be very effective framed and displayed.

The tawny owls look rather complicated, but as you study the picture and the actual shape of the birds, you will see the three dimensional form beginning to emerge. These lovely birds are brought to life by a careful selection of pieces for layering and feathering. Seven cards are required to create an attractive and detailed picture.

Cut around the outline of the birds. Feather cut outside edges, (see page 14), and darken with a pencil. Shape the edges on the wrong side with the tool foot so that they curve away from you. This is the first stage of building up the form. As the two birds are so similar, I will only work on layering up one of them. The owl on the left has more detail, so I will work on him, or her!

Before you begin, take note of the feet and claws at the front of the picture; they are covered by the lower body feathers. To re-create the three dimensional effect of feet grasping the branch, and at the appropriate stage during the layering process, make long feather cuts on these lower body feathers, and over-cut the claws from another print. The completed owl will be placed behind the branch and the lower body feathering will be shaped upwards to overlap the top of the partially hidden feet on the branch.

Now work on the soft down chest feathers. The owl will look more realistic if this section is cut into four parts. Use the most obvious natural lines from under the head to the feet, over-cutting into sections and heavily feathering edges. This will give the impression of real feathers overlapping each other.

The long flight feathers of the wing are over-cut and split into four sections. Split up the longest flight feathers into individual feathers, always remembering to over-cut where necessary and to feather exposed edges. Build up the flight feathers from the side nearest the claw outwards. Too much depth when gluing in position will look wrong, as the branch will have to be placed in position over these sections.

The shorter wing feathers can also be cut into four sections. If you wish, each of the prominent feathers may be over-cut, feather cut and layered up. If you cut out sections, rather than individual feathers, choose your cutting lines with care, seeking out the most natural break lines.

The head is worked on in a very similar way, but with a different emphasis on the shaping. In this instance the eyes do not really benefit from being cut out, whereas the owl will take on a natural look if the white feathers and beak are cut out and shaped over the face as a final touch. I have cut the head into three sections: the circular feathering around the eyes, another smaller, distinctly shaped circle of feathering around the eyes, and the white feathers and beak in between the eyes. Deep cutting into the white feathers is needed so they do not look too heavy or obvious.

When you cut the branches out, darken them along their edges and distinctly shape them, accentuating their curves and roundness. Some pressing with the craft tool, so as to give an embossed look where the bark is rough, adds a touch of authenticity.

The feet and claws should be cut out and placed on the branch and carefully tucked under the lower feathers as described previously. If you are enjoying the fine detailed work, you can add an extra dimension by cutting out and layering the claws.

***Tawny talk by Trevor Parkin**: the simple feather cutting technique is clearly visible in this picture of two tawny owls. Individual feathers are cut out and shaped to enhance realism and the branches of the tree stand out beautifully against the subdued background.*

Prickly subject

This subject is appealing because of the colours and subjects, and also because the outlines are strong and definite. Six cards are required to give a beautifully realistic finish.

Cut out the whole picture, including the trailing flower stems and leaves, but where items are small or extremely detailed, it is better to leave them out, rather than having ragged or thickly cut sections of fine detail.

Next, cut out the flowers and leaves behind the watering can, even though some stems twine around the handle. Shade, shape and glue in position.

Over-cut out the spout using a new card. Shade and gently shape to a gentle curve over the shaft of the craft tool. As the spout needs little height, use only enough glue to stick it in position.

The base picture is used to create an impression of depth within the watering can. So, the next section to cut out is the actual body of the can. Cut all round the sides, over-cutting where necessary, from the spout right round to under the hedgehog. Shade the edges. Shaping is important on this section because the can comes from the background, right round to the foreground, only to disappear again into the back of the scene. Fortunately, the hedgehog and leaves obliterate the distance on the right of the picture! Shape this section with your fingers and the tool shaft. Round the edge next to the spout and leave the darkened area fairly flat, only raised up with glue slightly. If this section is raised too high, it will be difficult to fit the cover and open lid on to the gaping top edge of the watering can later on. Bend the highlighted area of the can round quite distinctly. Shape around the edge of the far right section, so that it only curves over along the cut edge. Only a tiny amount of glue is required to give minimum height, as there is so much more detail to be placed over this section. Before gluing, keep placing the shaped section over the base picture, until it is at the best angle from the point of view of perspective. If you feel unhappy about the edges being short of the base picture because of the shaping, don't forget they will eventually be covered with flowers and leaves.

The cover and open lid are straightforward, so follow the usual procedure. When you reach the carrying handle, things may appear a little complicated at first glance because the handle twists in the middle. The solution is simple. Cut out the whole handle and the fixing bracket. Shade, shape and glue into place. Cut out the nearside section, omitting the fixing bracket, and taper the top to a finely cut point where the handle twists. Shape and glue in position so the finely cut point meets the corresponding top of the handle. Only raise the handle up as it curves round at its widest part and down to the fixing bracket. You can use the craft tool to its utmost here; raise up the riveting, the curved edges of handles and the brackets, almost embossing the paper to accentuate shapes.

The hedgehog is built up using similar techniques to those shown in the bird projects earlier in this book. Five layers, including the base layer, will give the best result. If you look closely at the picture you will notice a lightening of the spines in the central area of the hedgehog's back; this is suitable for the second layer. When you cut this section out, do not cut into the soft furry tummy, or head of the hedgehog, as this part of the picture can be used later on. Feather cut and shade the top edge. The inside edge will be overlaid with the next section. Shape curves, following the line of the spine and glue in position. Repeat this procedure again with another back section, using the illustration as a guide.

Prickly subject by David Blackmore*: flowers twine themselves around an abandoned watering can, whilst an inquisitive hedgehog discovers an unusual hiding place. This charming project illustrates a variety of cutting and shaping techniques.*

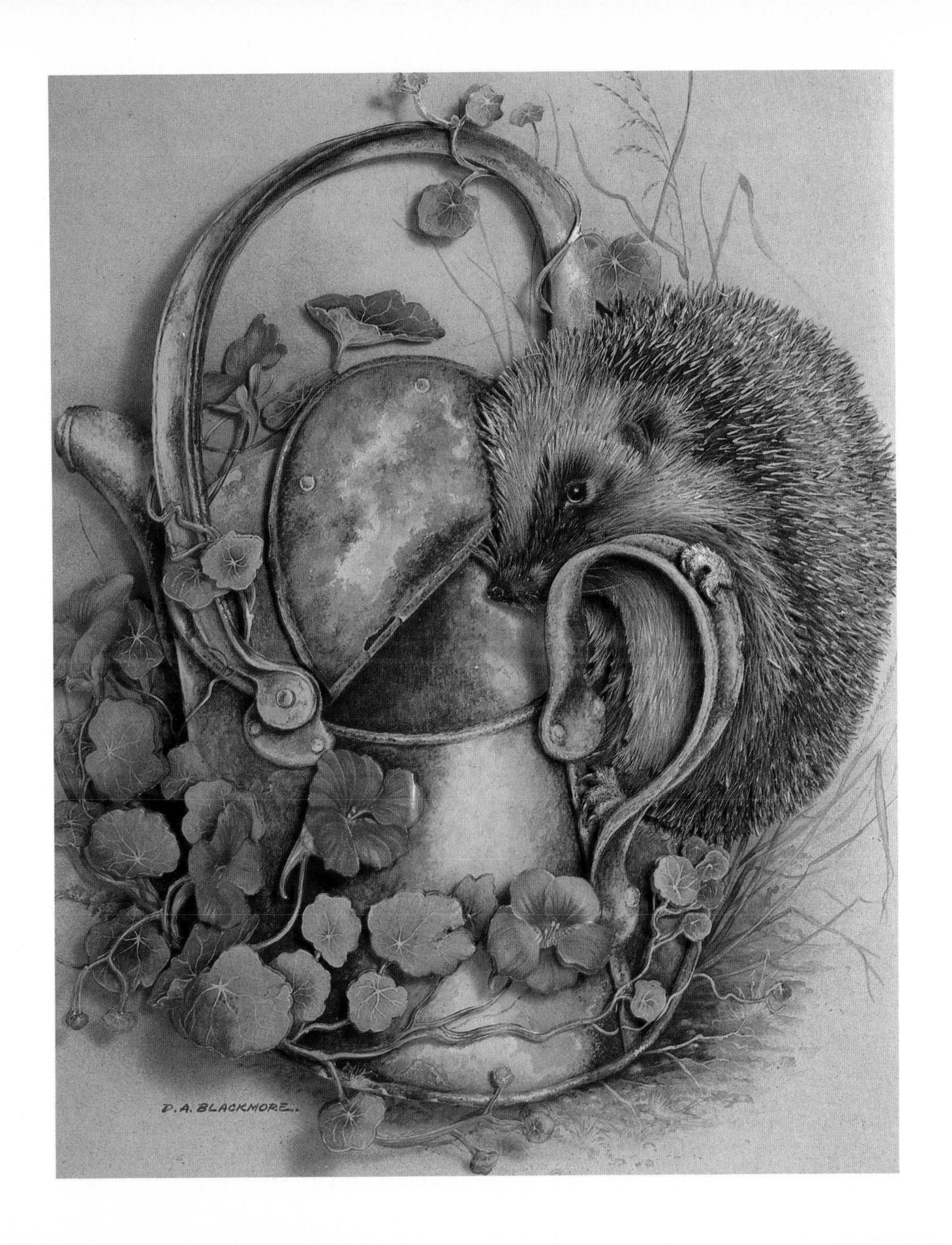
D.A. BLACKMORE

Over-cut out the back foot and glue in position. Cut the furry tummy into two sections, feather cutting edges and using the tool to accentuate the ear and eye. The last tummy section should include the nose and dark fur around the top of the eye. The cut line for the remaining fur can be positioned behind the pouring handle. Cut out and shape the pouring handle in the same way as the carrying handle, then glue in position before cutting out and attaching the shaped paw.

Now you can add the tangle of flowers and leaves. It is more effective if you can cut some of the stems out, and the flowers when layered up will add to the overall depth and beauty of this picture.

Autumn kitten

Some subjects look their best when removed from their original background and placed on a picture backing board of a contrasting, or complementary colour, as with this little kitten. If you prefer to complete this delightful picture in this way a minimum of five cards are required. However, should you want to use the complete picture as a mount, then six cards are needed; also if you want to incorporate a great deal of detail, seven cards are required.

To begin, cut out the whole kitten, then feather cut and shade the edges all the way round. The kitten is shaped round the edges using the tool so that the whole body has a slight convex finished form. At this stage there is no need to shape any individual parts as this first cut out is overlaid by later sections of the kitten when building up the picture.

The first section to cut out is the tail, beneath the plant leaf. It needs to be feather cut and shaped so that the tip is bending over and downwards, the whole tail having a convex shape. Glue the tail into position on the main base kitten.

Next, cut out the back paw between the tail tip and the front paws. Over-cut this section, making sure that you cut into the front paw, so that the cut line will be hidden. Naturally, the cut lines round the back paw will show, but they should be darkened with pencil, feathering the toes where they meet the path, and leaving the upper darkened outline of the paw smooth. Shape and glue into position. Do not raise the back paw up too much but visualise that it is, in fact, farther away from you than the tip of the tail or front paws.

Now cut out the chest; that small part of the kitten's coat in between the front legs. Over-cut out this part well into the front legs and up into the darker band of fur between the chin and the top of the legs. No feathering, or darkening of edges, is needed here; just some good shaping. You can see from the picture that the fur on the chest stands out, so you will need to shape this section in a pronounced convex. Do make sure that it is only the part of the chest actually showing that stands out, otherwise you will have difficulty gluing the legs in position. Glue this section into place; at first glance it may not appear to make a great deal of difference. If you look at the picture, however, you will observe that the chest is obviously farther forward than the back section between the tail and the rear paw. What you have done is to create the correct perspective.

You now need to cut out the legs and will immediately feel that, at last, something more creative is happening! Begin cutting out from the light ruff under the chin. Cut a gap where the chest section is, but keep the front paws together, thus forming a V shape. Feather cut round the legs and front paws. Shape the whole section, paying particular attention to the paws which should stand out in a slight hump. Glue into position. Don't lose heart at this stage, it will look awful!

Now to build up the fur from the top of the front legs, and this is where you may want to put in more time and effort. Cut out a section from the top of the legs, using the fur bands as a cutting line, making sure that it will cover the cut line of the V section of legs and paws. Cut right up to the ears and feather cut the fur *inside* the ears; cut off any feathery fur from the back of the ears and the dark fur at the top of the head. In effect you are cutting out the head, neck and top of the chest in one slightly smaller section. This has two advantages. It brings into play the perspective of the kitten and actually increases the three dimensional effect because in the final picture you will see the back layer. Feather cut and shade edges. Shape so that feathered edges curve towards the base picture and glue in position.

Over-cut out the bib section under the head, cutting the sides smaller and feather cutting so that it blends in with the last layer of fur. Darken edges, shape and glue in position.

Cut out the head, but only cut out the fur that overlaps the ears and cut out the forehead, again slightly lower than before. Feather cut the head all around, with long, deep cuts, paying particular attention to the whiskers and fur in front of ears. Shaping is important here. Shape in a convex as before, but heavily outline the dark rim above the eyes and the curve of the mouth (for this technique see the method for shaping leaf veins on page 16). There will now be an embossed raised line over each eye and around the mouth. Glue the head in position, making sure that the angle is correct, with the kitten looking up. Cut out the little pink nose, darken edges, shape and glue in position, but do not raise up. This small detail does not need any height except the paper thickness of itself.

Cut out a few leaves and the flower. Proceed in the normal way, finally gluing into position. The leaves may also be layered to create depth.

***Autumn kitten by Ernest Hyde**: this appealing long-haired kitten is an ideal subject. The fur is feather cut and layered to create a realistic effect. To give a greater feeling of depth the autumn leaves and flowers are also cut out and layered.*

1

2

3

4

The love letter

Seven cards are required for this picture, (see page 5). Cut out the girl, over-cutting where necessary. You will need to cut into the gatepost, and carefully cut around her waist where her arm, waist and gatepost top meet. Shade the edges of the figure and shape so they curve over slightly. You will build up on this base.

Step 1: Over-cut out the foot and ankle in the foreground, making sure you cut well into the hem of the skirt. Shade, shape and glue in position. Now, carefully cut out the shoe, putting a little more emphasis on the shaping, particularly where the instep rises up. Glue it in position.

Step 2: Now layer up the two pink skirts. Cut out the pink hemline above the tuck in the skirt. Shade the edges, then shape the folds in the material, (see page 17). After you have glued this section in position, use the card that you cut the ankle and foot from and over-cut out the second layer of the skirt. You will need to cut into the gatepost and the apron, but only cut from the bottom of the tuck. Shade, shape fold lines and glue in position.

Step 3: Cut out the apron and shape fold lines as before, taking care not to crease the paper. Glue in position. Cut out the arm holding the letter, but only the sleeve; do not cut at the wrist or hand. Avoid cutting through sections that you may need later on. Follow the previous stages of shading, shaping and positioning.

Step 4: remember that you are always working from the back of the subject, so in this case, the front of the girl's blouse is the next section. The cutting line is going to run through many other sections that have yet to be used, so cut the section out from one of the used cards. Work from left to right and cut through the sleeve of the arm supporting the chin, the bonnet, across the face (avoid cutting through the hair), through the bonnet again, the white strap line of the apron, the hand holding the letter and across through the middle of the waistband on the apron. Darken exposed cutting line edges - the two tiny sections at the waist and shoulder. Shape, accentuating the puffiness of the blouse by curving the section over the tool shaft. Glue in position. Taking a new card, cut out the right hand bonnet section, as you look at the picture, the straps of the apron and the waist-band, all in one piece. Shade edges and shape using the tool shaft so that this awkward piece will sit well over the picture. Glue carefully in position.

Step 5: over-cut out the face, cutting into the bonnet and hair. Shade and shape, accentuating the nose and eyebrows. Glue carefully in position, matching the face angle with the angle painted in the picture.

Step 6: over-cut out the section of hair and feather cut the top edges. When gluing this section, leave the hair standing away from the paper slightly, so that when the bonnet is positioned the small areas behind the hair can be tucked out of sight.

Step 7: cut the bonnet out, leaving the right hand section as this piece has already been cut out in a previous stage. Shape and glue in position.

Step 8: carefully cut round the arm and hand supporting the chin. When you have completed this stage, cut out the sleeve, arm and hand holding the letter. Carefully shape the sleeve edge, accentuating the outline. Glue in place, leaving the fingers and hand raised up so that the letter can be placed on to the hand and set back slightly.

5

6

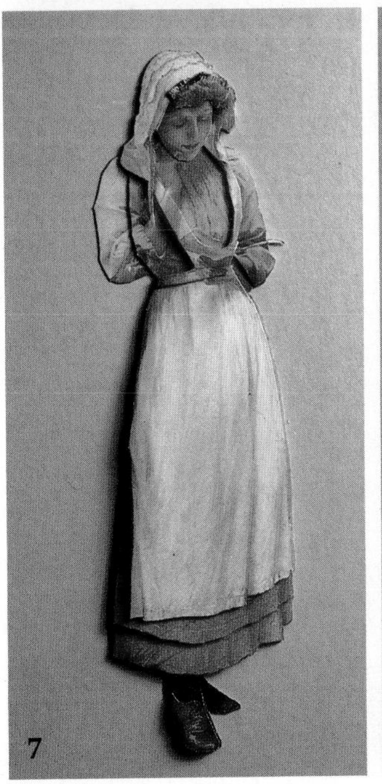
7

8

The finished figure: finally, to complete the figure, cut out the letter and the upper sleeve to the cuff and forearm supporting the chin. When cutting the sleeve you have to cut into the top of the gatepost. The gatepost can be added to the finished picture, as we have shown in the completed illustration. Shade and shape, accentuating the cuff end of the sleeve and glue both the letter and the sleeve in position.

The background to this charming figure has also been layered up, using techniques described earlier in this book. The full picture can be seen on page 5.

***The love letter by Charles Edward Wilson**: creating a beautifully detailed picture like this is extremely rewarding and the more work you put into it, the better the end result will be. Careful shaping of folds of material will enhance the three dimensional effect.*

***Orphans by Charles Edward Wilson**: This rustic scene springs charmingly to life using just a few simple layering and shaping techniques.*

Orphans

The picture on the previous page, showing a young boy feeding the orphan lambs, is a lovely figure study with some interesting features. When creating three dimensional figures it is advisable to commence by cutting out the whole figure, working at the layering up process on this main cut out section. After completion it can then be glued into place on the main picture. Six cards, including a backing card, are required for this project.

I like to begin at the feet and work upwards towards the head. In this instance the first items to cut out are the shoes. These are cut out together in one piece, allowing an over-cut so that when the leggings are placed in position, they obviously overlap the top of the shoes.

Cut out the leggings in one piece, over-cutting the tops into the smock; shape and glue in position. Before the smock is cut out, the half hidden arm holding the turnip should be cut out and positioned.

When cutting out the smock, or any clothes, dark folds at the back will be visible on the main base figure giving a feeling of depth and reality. Shape the folds in the material; larger sections such as the smock always benefit from additional shaping, so accentuate the folds and edges.

Now cut out the boy's head. This is an obvious choice for the next layer because his neck is behind the neckerchief and the smock collar, even though his face is actually leaning forwards. You will achieve the correct angle for the face by shaping and tilting the head section when gluing in place, with the front of the face slightly higher than the back of the neck.

The red spotted neckerchief is the next section for layering. If you find this item is too small to cut out on its own, do not worry; it can easily be cut out with the collar section in one piece and well shaped to create the illusion of layers. This is often advisable when small areas of a picture are overlapped by other areas. In the illustration, I have cut out the collar and the neckerchief separately.

The arm holding the knife and the hand holding the turnip make up the next layer. In the illustration, the hand and cuff holding the knife were cut out in one piece; then the sleeve from the wrist to the shoulder where the collar overlaps the top of the sleeve was cut out separately.

Finally, cut out the blue felt hat, shape and glue into place. It is well worth spending a little more time on a figure when it is the main subject of a picture.

The background scene has been layered to create a feeling of depth. Inside the barn the hay tumbles to the floor and feathered edges spill out into the yard. The horseshoe hangs at a crazy angle on the open door. The crook rests lazily against the side of the barn, while the plump little lambs munch happily away at the turnips. This charming scene would look extremely effective mounted on contrasting card and framed and displayed.

Green Bottom Farm, Embsay

This Yorkshire farm, with its neat angular buildings and solid stone walls bathed in sunlight, contrasts beautifully with the sky and moors beyond. The bare trees paint a bleaker picture and make the smoke from the farmhouse chimney, the open yard and bright red tractor a welcoming sight on a winter morning. Seven cards, including the backing card, are used to create this tranquil scene.

The trees immediately behind the farmhouse are cut out as a whole group, cutting around the tree trunks but leaving the branches and twigs as a whole section. It is important to shape the tree tops so they curve over towards the sky. This prevents the outlines from looking too harsh and obvious when the section is glued on to the backing card.

The far section of the yard wall is cut out next. This

Green Bottom Farm, Embsay by Alan Ingham*: the perspective and subject make this an interesting project. Careful assessment of the picture is essential when working on a scene like this.*

is shaped and glued in position cut out the farmhouse. Shape the edges and layer. If there is any doubt as to how the cut out section will look when glued in position, place it on the backing card before applying the glue, checking the shaping and assessing how much depth is required at this stage. Bear in mind that the stone walls at the front of the picture will lose their correct perspective if the items in the background are placed too high up from the base picture. As a general rule, it is better to create a smaller gap between layers to the rear of the picture, and a wider gap between layers in the foreground.

It is up to you how much detail you put into your picture. As a general guide the next section is the building with the sloping roof. Layer as usual.

Now cut out the road. This is an unusual feature because of its perspective and it became evident early on in the building up process, that unless the road was cut out and tilted up at the extreme front of the picture, the perspective would be lost. Consequently the walls and buildings would appear to be falling out of the picture! Cut out the section through both walls on either side of the picture and through the tractor in the centre. Shape the pavement on the right hand side to make it stand out and glue the section in position, raising up the front edge slightly with the glue. Now cut out the tractor and position it over the cut line.

The next section is the barn on the right of the yard, followed by the wall around the house and yard. Then in the foreground layer the terraced house, shed and large tree on the left, the long curved wall and finally the terraced house walls. Shape and glue all these sections in position.

On rather difficult looking sections, where a greater degree of depth is required due to the perspective of the picture, it is wise to keep the lower edge of the section almost touching the base picture; for example the bottom of the walls should touch the ground, so only a small gap is needed, otherwise the sections will look as though they are suspended in mid-air! However, due to the perspective of this picture, a degree of depth is needed between layers. The solution is to create a wider gap between layers at the top of the section with the glue. This means the section will be tilted farther out at the top than the bottom.

In the case of the large stone wall curving towards the farm buildings, this cut out section is tilted in two directions: top and bottom, with more height at the top, and at the beginning and end of the wall, with more height in the foreground. This then gives the correct perspective, with the wall curving down the road towards the farm entrance. It is interesting to note how the stone walls draw the eye to the red tractor in the centre of the picture.

This was an interesting project and I enjoyed the challenge of the perspective. I hope the techniques you have learnt here will inspire you to create many more scenes.

Cottage garden

Scenes are a tempting subject, but they have one obvious drawback and that is the distance, or perspective, that is encompassed in the picture. You cannot, for example, cut out a tree on a distant hillside and a shrub in the foreground, without losing the illusion of distance, or causing the foreground subjects to be built up so high with glue, that they look awkward. In this picture the distant trees, the hedge, fencing and trees behind the cottages have not been cut out, because the distance from them to the little watering can in the foreground is far too great for the layering process. Five cards are required to complete this charming picture.

Although it is a very busy scene with the most

***Cottage garden* by John H. Tyson**: *very little shaping is needed in this picture. Banks of flowers are built up aginst a simple background and the three dimensional effect is created by a simple layering process.*

beautiful array of flowers, it is easier to create than a scene with barely any detail. The only shaping necessary is on the cottages. The roof windows can be accentuated. Also a little feather cutting around thatched roof corners adds a touch of authenticity and charm.

The first layer is the group of garden flowers just in front of the hedge and fencing. This section takes in the beehives, the tall delphiniums and the lean-to resting on the farthest cottage. Note that when you cut out a section in a scene like this, you only need to over-cut slightly. For example, when cutting out the cottages, only cut out enough to ensure that overlapped edges are hidden. Cut out this first section, shade and glue in position.

The next layer is made up of several items; the farthest cottage with the doorways cut out, the small delphiniums in front of the lean-to and the front beehive. Shade, shape and position the sections.

The third layer is made up of part of the hedge, the large clump of delphiniums in front of the open door, and the daisies. Also, the cottage in the foreground is cut out at this stage. This is the only time this cottage is cut out and the doorway is cut as an open gap.

Now the front bay window of the cottage and the two climbing roses are cut out and layered, as are the delphiniums by the doorway. This creates the fourth layer, but as these items have not been cut out before, any prominence that is required is achieved by the amount of glue used.

The white flowers under the bay window, the red daisies, evergreen shrub and adjacent white blossoms, (not the lilies), are all cut out in one piece to create the fifth layer. Also cut out the top clump of pink daisies, poppies and yellow blooms in the left foreground; in this case over-cut the section. Layer as before.

The flowers behind the path edging are at the same level, or glued height. Cut from the top of the lilies in the centre in both directions, following the line of the tops of the flowers. Make sure that the line of flowers dwindles down towards the end of the path.

The next layer is made up of the path, path edging and the flowers in the right foreground of the picture.

Now, to complete the picture, cut out in one section the flowers in the left foreground. Do not forget the little watering can in the very front of the picture!

Tailpiece

By now you will feel more confident about tackling the subjects illustrated in this book, so I have only given general guidelines to help you create this dear little mouse. Seven cards are required, including the base card.

Our mouse looks very simple to do, as indeed he is, but you will need a little guidance in the layering up process of his tummy and his long pink tail, because of the problem of perspective.

To begin, cut out the main base figure, then layer up the front foot and back thigh, and the ears, head and face at the same time, always checking the perspective and over-cutting where necessary. Feather cut all exposed furry edges.

Cut out the exposed fur around the tops of the ears to add to the feeling of depth. As you can see in the illustration opposite, I have cut out the mouth which adds to the feeling of realism. On the layer above the base layer, cut out the area between the teeth and the tongue. On the top layer, cut out the whole mouth section and shape the bottom lip. The eyes and the nose are well shaped to add life and definition. The

Tailpiece by Gilly.

lower face is also cut out; cut a clean edge along the top of the cheeks, over the little pink nose from ear to ear, and position.

The rounded cream coloured tummy needs a little more explanation. This section is in front of the back thigh and foot, and behind the front thigh, arms and tail. You will notice that the tummy fur overlaps the front thigh. Before gluing the tummy and front thigh and body sections into place fit them together, almost as if you are pushing two combs together, teeth to teeth. Position the feathered creamy tummy fur over the brown thigh and body, making sure that the thigh overlaps the lower tummy section. Shape and glue these sections into place as one piece.

The pink tail also needs careful consideration. You will see that it comes from the back of the picture, right round to the front! This appears to throw out of the window all my previous instructions of working from the back of the picture in layers. You will have to create the illusion of perspective, but this is not as difficult as it appears. Cut out the tail and darken the edges as usual. When you shape the tail, only curve over the end at the back; if the tail is shaped too much it will never match the picture below. It will need to be glued in position after the main body sections and before the arms, but before attaching keep checking that it looks correct and matches up at the top and base tips. It may need kinking slightly under the arms, where a slight crease will not show, so that it matches.

As an amusing touch a few strands of hair can be used for the whiskers as they are slightly springy, although I have not used anything. Thread of a similar colour would also work quite well. When attaching, place the glue on the strands of thread, rather than on the picture.

Always remember that this is a personal craft and there is no right or wrong way of creating your picture, as long as you are happy with the result!

I hope the projects in this book will inspire you to experiment and create many more beautiful pictures and gifts.

First published in Great Britain 1989
Search Press Limited
Wellwood, North Farm Road,
Tunbridge Wells, Kent TN2 3DR

Photographs Search Press Studios

The illustrations in this book are reproduced by kind permission of Royle Publications Limited, Royle House, Wenlock Road, London N1 7ST The publishers would like to thank them for their help and cooperation.

The author would like to thank Royle Publications for supplying the cards shown in this book, her husband for all his help and encouragement and Mr Graham Spite of Courtyard Gallery, Kirtons Farm Country Club, Pingewood, Reading, for the frame surrounding the 'Cottage Garden' shown on page 22.

ISBN 0 85532 621 2

Typeset by Scribe Design, 123 Watling Street, Gillingham, Kent
Made and printed in Spain by A. G. Elkar, S. Coop.-48012-Bilbao.